I0492702

Blockchain

Understanding Blockchain Technology and Cryptocurrency

information is without contract or any type of guarantee assurance.

The trademarks that are used are without any consent, and the publication of the trademark is without permission or backing by the trademark owner. All trademarks and brands within this book are for clarifying purposes only and are owned by the owners themselves, not affiliated with this document.

Table of Contents

Introduction

The human race as a whole is now developing at a much faster rate than at any other time in history. This is due partly to most people's access to better nutrition, partly because people in general have access to a better standard of education, but mainly because the advances being made in technology and communication are opening up the world.

Communication, understanding how it works and how to implement all the new developments as they happen in this vast field is crucial for all in the new world.

The age of communication is here now. People entering the workforce who want to be top earners and achievers need a thorough understanding of the new forms of communication such as blockchain and cryptocurrency.

It has long been accepted that knowledge is power and the more knowledge you have, the more control and leverage you have over your life, work, others, and circumstances.

Knowing how to use or apply the knowledge you gain is the key to success. Many people also know that too much knowledge, in the hands of the wrong people, can be very dangerous. This is one of the reasons blockchain is so important. It is available for all people to see, to check and add to from their computer. When a post is made and embedded in the blockchain, it becomes irreversible and unchangeable.

It was only just over 400 years ago, in 1600, that William Gilbert, a physician in the English court of Queen Elizabeth the first, revealed to the world his discovery of electricity. When he published his findings and research about this new discovery, "electrica" the world was forever changed and plunged into the modern age of electricity.

It started slowly, taking until 1792 for the first long distance semaphore telegraph line to be established by Claude Chappe. This was a system of using pivoting shutters to send visual signals and information in the form of coded messages.

Then, 243 years more, before Samuel Morse built the first long distance electric telegraph. Suddenly, long range almost instant communication was possible with the Morse code.

33 years later in 1876, Thomas A. Watson and Alexander Graham Bell exhibit the electric telephone for the first time sending the human voice along telephone lines.

Once knowledge of electricity and how to apply it had become more common, new discoveries and inventions such as the phonograph, the radio, movie pictures, television, automobiles, electric trains, airplanes and a host of other inventions suddenly arrived.

With the first and second world wars, by necessity, many new developments were discovered such as radar, atomic science, microelectronics, and computers. The old cumbersome valve operated equipment was replaced with transistors and microchips, allowing electronics to become smaller and more powerful.

Advances in electronics and communication continues up until today. Now, everyone can effortlessly carry their own perfectly clear mass communication systems with them everywhere.

The beginning of the Internet 30 years ago was a huge leap forward for humanity. It brought another new age of mass communication to most parts of the world. Now the Internet has become affordable and reliable for everyone, many people could not live without it. In fact, many people's livelihoods and businesses are dependent on the Internet.

Now about half the people in the world have Internet access, it is estimated in the US about 87% of people from school age up have regular Internet contact. The 13% without Internet is largely made up of people over 65 and those on the lowest incomes in remote country areas.

The latest Internet figures suggest that there are 3.8 billion people actively using the Internet every day, with another 38 million signing up every six months. The majority of non-users are in Africa, India, China and other eastern countries.

It is hard to determine how many people actively use blockchain today. Currently, it's estimated that there are over 35 million people signed on to the new blockchain sites blockchain.org and bitcoin.

The Internet has many positive features and its use is growing in areas all over the world. Unfortunately, because of the way the Internet is structured, it is open to misrepresentations, misuse, corruption and fraud. This is mainly due to the fact there are just so many people using the Internet at any one time, it is impossible to keep track of things. This makes it reasonably easy for hackers, scammers and fraudsters to steal information and operate illegally.

The lack of built in security in the Internet has created limitations on its use. There are many areas that could have benefited much more from the Internet, areas such as security and government departments, taxation and finance. These areas have had restricted or limited growth in many of these sensitive areas because it is impossible to realistically authenticate and track all its many users.

The reason for this is because the Internet is a system of closed files that are "posted" and then stored in huge computer centers that hold billions of pieces of individual information.

All this information is used and monetized by the intermediaries. The individual people using the net do not have any control over what is actually their intellectual property. A good example of this is Google, Facebook, and the other social media platforms. They may be free to use, but when you enter your personal details or post items, they can be and are used to collect information about you.

Any intermediary that you use, such as government departments, banks, e-commerce or technology companies are able to use this information or sell it. Sometimes, they use it to keep track of our spending and buying habits so they can refine advertising campaigns, sometimes to detect new market trends. Often it is used to help companies directly personalize targeted advertising campaigns at individuals because it records your preferences and shopping history.

Blockchain is fundamentally different to the Internet as it now stands and removes the need for intermediaries of all kinds. Any institution regardless of whether public, like government departments or private, such as banks, insurance, any agency that governs any transactions between any two people or entities and then stores their information will become practically obsolete.

What makes blockchain so different is that it works completely the opposite way to the existing Internet. All the data, every comment, every transaction, each webpage or website, each click or search we generate, in fact, every action remains ours and under our control. It is stored in blocks and secured with cryptography; it is time and date stamped and totally traceable. All the actions you take with blockchain are and always will remain the property of you, its author and once validated, it cannot be changed or removed.

The Internet now is basically about information sharing but in the form of content. Blockchain is about sharing and storing anything of value in an open-source decentralized database. This database records every transaction and action on a block, with all blocks linked to the other blocks. This is why it is called blockchain.

The practical application is that when someone wishes to use the concept of peer to peer sharing (The idea of exchanging or bartering goods or services directly with another), using blockchain, everything is simplified resulting in no middleman. This is reflected in person to person transaction, often resulting in a reduced price with both parties receive better value.

This is a concept that horrifies and terrifies big corporations, banks, and insurance companies. This is because, by and large, these types of businesses are only middlemen who live off others. Sometimes they take a larger share of other people's endeavors such as wholesalers and retailers who often realize more profit than the original grower or developer. Sometimes, like bankers, they take only a little from a lot of people or loan the same money to many to compound their return.

When you have to pay or barter for a service or product you require, instead of using a check, credit/debit card or online transfer and passing on your details to the bank or financial institution, you can keep it to yourself. This can be done by allowing the other person or party to just directly take the payment (whether monetary, assets or services) from your blockchain. All it takes is to provide them with a password/code that validates and allows them to access the agreed amount and they can be paid by direct access on blockchain.

An easy way to visualize blockchain is to picture a honeycomb, a giant honeycomb with each cell or "block" locked together. This honeycomb is then running on every device that is in the system, everywhere in the world.

Blockchain technology is forcing many changes in how the world deals with money, business and many worldly things and concepts. This includes intellectual property, different forms of new and existing technology, science and discovery, research and exploration.

Blockchain can even be used for diverse things like voting in elections by counting and ensuring the validity of voters. Checking or screening people at immigration and ports of entry can also use blockchain. It can be a major help in the fight to eradicate the threat of terrorism and crime in general.

Blockchain can also be used for trading at any time on the stock market or any financial market or produce market at any time, after hours.

Blockchain, like the Internet and some areas of it, blockchain is not owned by anyone, any single company or even any government. No one owns the data, you are not dependent on a company giving you conditions and being able to sanction your input. No one can censor your Blockchain. Of course, you can censor or control your own area and what you allow yourself and your family to come into contact with on blockchain, but that is another story.

Blockchain gives you the option to have all your details and documents setup and ready, so if you need to make a transaction that needs those details, they are there instantly. If you want to open a bank account, renew your passport, buy a cell phone or get a drivers or gun license all these can be done on blockchain, without the hassle of waiting in line or dealing with interviews.

Blockchain is unlikely to totally replace the net as we know it, but it has and will keep on modifying it as some types of Internet interaction are best suited to a centralized database like today's Internet, while many other functions are entirely appropriate for blockchain.

One huge advantage blockchain has over the current Internet is it allows different parties who do not really trust each other to be able to trade without the fear of being compromised of defrauded, simply because all blockchain transactions are so open and incorruptible.

This is because all blockchain processes are done by a network of users that act as a consensus mechanism. This ensures that everyone using blockchain has the same shared system, a system of incorruptible record simultaneously.

Banks work because they have earned through their actions a certain amount of trust. Their depositors trust them to keep their money secure and to pay a dividend or interest for the use of that money.

Almost all financial institutions, including banks, up until very recently, have used private databases or centralized database systems. The main problem with these systems is that anybody who has sufficient access to these systems (whether legally or fraudulently obtained) can easily destroy or corrupt the data that these systems contain.

This makes the people who use these systems depend on the honesty of the system's administrators. It also makes it necessary to spend vast amounts, often billions of dollars collectively to keep these centrally held databases or systems from being corrupted, altered by hackers or attacked by anyone else wishing to profit from other people's losses.

If the central administrators and or their databases become corrupted then it is the customers, the people who borrow and lend money via these systems that become the eventual losers.

Many systems such as PayPal, Bankcard, Visa, and Western Union still use their traditional database, digital transaction technology systems. The main reason they have not changed over is that they are much faster than blockchain at the moment.

Blockchain is still developing and improving, many companies are keeping a close eye on these new developments as they will soon enhance blockchain speed and performance without sacrificing security. Once this happens, it is expected blockchain will become the leading platform used by all financial institutions worldwide.

Distributed networks that use blockchain do not have or use shared or compound processing, they are each totally independent of any service network. Instead, each blockchain individually services the network, then it compares the results of its computations with other blockchain and the rest of the net until it finds a consensus of a particular happening.

Now the world is entering a new phase of communication and commerce with Blockchain Technology, a new form of Internet that is incorruptible.

The Internet as we know it today is made up of many individual files that are closed or locked to everyone except the originator or persons with the originator's permission. Sometimes the owner or originator of these files will make access to these files open to anyone for viewing only with limited interaction available unless someone has the access codes.

All standard Internet files including websites, web pages, and emails all have content that can be true, false, misleading or malicious, depending on what the author decided to publish on or in them. They are also able to be stolen or copied.

Blockchain is the complete opposite, due to its nature, it is incorruptible. It is self-checking and self-regulating and open to everyone. Blockchain will not accept false information because, in order for it to be accepted, it must first be checked by all the blocks in the chain.

Chapter 1: History of Blockchain

How did it come about and who invented it?

The beginnings of blockchain started with the work of W. Scott Starletta and Stuart Haber when they were working on a cryptographically secure chain of blocks in 1991.

Blockchain as we know it now was devised as a method for using a digital currency called Bitcoin by Satoshi-Takemoto. Whether Satoshi-Takemoto is an actual person or a group of people who are computer science and cryptography experts from Europe and The Americas is open to speculation and dispute.

Blockchain is a form of computer code. When it was first released in 2008, its primary purpose was to allow bitcoins, a form of digital currency, to be distributed without allowing them to be copied, making them absolutely safe and incorruptible. This was largely as a response to the financial crisis in 2008. During this time there was a strong free software culture movement in support of the ideals of anti-establishmentism, with some strong anti-commercial values.

This is largely why it was developed by the public sector and not private enterprises like the financial institutions which, if they were the ones to develop it would have had a stranglehold on it and excluded everyone else from gaining access.

This new technology is the backbone of a different type of Internet that has an infinite range of new application possibilities in all areas of communication and commerce.

One of the best applications for blockchain is in peer to peer transactions that exclude any form of middleman. Using cyber currency such as bitcoin, the dollar value it holds is secure, bitcoin can only be spent once, the value can be moved, but it is not possible to double spend bitcoin.

Bitcoin is 100% traceable, it can be seen where it came from and where it goes from you to the next destination. It is impossible to hide it or launder it in the usual sense.

If someone was able to steal a bitcoin, its value would just be removed, making it worthless, so under normal circumstances, it is theft proof.

From its inception in 2008 to August 2014, the bitcoin blockchain grew to a file size of 20 gigabytes, by February 2015 it had grown to 30 gigabytes. It reached 50 gigabytes in January 2016 and then 100 gigabytes by January 2017, it is currently about 160 gigabytes.

There are other blockchains such as Ethereum Blockchain, it started at the beginning of 2016 and has been growing at a phenomenal speed.

In July 2016, it had grown to 25 gigabytes, in October of that year it was just over 50 gigabytes. By January 2017, it had grown to 130 gigabytes and now has passed bitcoin by 40% reaching 180 plus gigabytes and is expected to reach 1 terabyte in 2018.

Blockchain has now a version called "Blockchain.2." A new application of blockchain distributed database. This new version has a second generation programming language that allows people to write smart contracts. These contracts can pay themselves when a job is completed or a shipment arrives at its destination. Share certificates can be issued that have the ability to pay dividends when they reach a predetermined amount or value.

These abilities allow all people to enter the global economy. Regardless of race, creed, color or religious conviction, people will be able to compete on their merits and the quality of their work. Blockchain brings together people who would otherwise have been unable to do business together. All farmers and producers can have the ability to deal directly with the consumer and those consumers are able to ascertain how and under what conditions the produce they are buying was grown or caught.

This also applies to artists and creators of both physical and purely emotional works, they can protect their intellectual property. Blockchain can be used by the music industry to collect royalties, stop piracy and manage copyrights.

Chapter 2: What is Blockchain Simplified

In very simple terms, blockchain could be described as a digital ledger or decentralized database. A safe place to store all types of transactions that everyone can use and have access to anytime.

Most people and businesses do the majority of their transactions using a middleman, a trusted third party to hold the money so to speak, such as a bank or other financial institution. Blockchain removes the need for a middleman and allows buyers, consumers, and suppliers to connect directly with one another. It has the potential to do away with cash and work directly with what the asset's cash represents.

Cash or "legal tender" like US Dollars is really just a medium of exchange for the purchase of property, goods or services, a medium that has a recognized exchange value.

Paper money "notes" and currency in a country was once linked directly to the gold standard. The country would hold a reserve of gold equal to the currency in circulation and its value was determined by the world price of gold.

In America, between 1879 and 1933 you could have traded $20.67 for an ounce of pure gold in your bank. This was stopped when President F. Roosevelt abandoned the gold standard in 1933 in order to combat the Great Depression.

In 1971, President Nixon stopped foreign governments from exchanging US Dollars for gold, because while doing so, they were depleting America's gold reserves. Nixon then completely severed America's remaining links between gold and the dollar.

Now in the US and many other countries, the value of a country's currency is determined by their gross national capital value, the value of the country's assets. This is a much more convenient system for blockchain.

Using blockchain, it would be possible for people to barter directly for good and services. For example, a dairy farmer may wish to purchase some clothes. Instead of the farmer selling his dairy products such as cheese, milk or butter to a distributor who sells to a retailer who then goes on to sell to the tailor, he goes online and views the tailor's wares directly. He makes his choice of clothes, they agree on an exchange or price and because there are no middlemen, both receive a 100% value from their own labor and the drastically reduced prices reflect the fact that there is no nonproductive element.

If the tailor does not want any dairy products, but wants fish, fuel for the car, or some other service or product then other applications or programs in blockchain can link the right buyers and sellers. By extension, this could be in other parts of the country or any country of the world.

This is the reason such people as Richard Branson, Bill Gates and others along with bankers and insurance companies worldwide are desperately trying to become the first to work out how to master and control it.

The theory is that blockchain technology could work with or for just about any transaction, including money, goods and services, futures, stocks, bonds and gambling.

The potential uses for blockchain are really limitless. It can be used for accounting purposes, projecting income and probability levels, collecting and or the paying of taxes, assessing wages or payments, calculation of costs and expenses, calculus, as well as doing banking transactions where banking facilities are difficult or unavailable.

One of the incredible features of blockchain is it is open and transparent, every transaction is open and recorded in a public ledger that everyone can see, it cannot be hidden or corrupted.

Blockchain also self-checks the facts and looks for any discrepancies or inaccuracies in the transaction or with the parties involved. This would most likely mean the transaction was not able to proceed until the problems detected were resolved or rectified. This virtually eliminates fraud and dishonesty.

One area this could be of great value in the insurance industry, it could allow most honest insurance claims to be instantly honored.

If you were to buy a secondhand car or another item, you could check its complete service record, its previous owners and ensure it was debt free.

Blockchain is a series, chain or network of computers that are linked together, it is very similar to today's Internet, but has a few important differences.

Blockchain can be any size required from a small personal blockchain that is meant only for a selected group such as members of your family, a sports club, the students in a classroom or the people working in your company. These types of blockchain are closed and can only be accessed by people specifically invited, those with the right codes.

Other blockchains can be huge and open to everyone, anywhere. These huge networks can contain blocks with an enormous amount of information; people would still need access codes in order to access the blockchain. But these codes are freely available for anyone, a person can apply to get and use the code and, in some instances, all it takes is to click on a button.

When any information is entered into the blockchain, it is automatically checked by all the other blocks in the chain by the computers in the network. They all have to approve it before it can be verified and recorded. This check can be almost instant or takes just a few moments depending on the amount of information and the size of the blockchain. It works in a similar way to using email or google search.

To get an idea of what blockchain is, it is helpful to think of it as being like a spreadsheet where you place all your data. A similar type of spreadsheet you can find in google docs. This spreadsheet can be made so that it will open to other people you have given access to or allowed in. You can decide just what actions each individual can do, such as allowing them to view only or view and interact by adding data.

Think how convenient this would be if others were able to contribute to the same document while you are also working on it. Imagine if all parties involved were able to work on a joint file working from different computers in possibly different locations (even countries) at the same time, in real time. Instead of each having their own copies of it and then each person having to update and send or exchange the spreadsheet with each of the other parties.

Consider how helpful a program on your spreadsheet would be that can check all the data being entered, verify it as being authentic, correct and accurate, before it is allowed to be added. This program would then automatically update itself every few minutes.

Add to this the ability to be able to ensure the true identity of all those using it, eliminating the possibilities of pretense, scamming and any type of Internet fraud.

Now think of this spreadsheet as being not private, but being open to everyone, where it is duplicated thousands or even millions of times across a vast network of computers, so everyone who is using it has to be open, honest, and transparent.

This will give you a basic understanding of what Blockchain is and an idea of some of the possibilities for its application.

A very good example is the way a normal business document or agreement gets processed:

- The first step is an idea is discussed verbally.
- Then, a business document is drafted.
- This document is then passed back and forth between all parties for agreement, comments, additions or subtractions, etc.
- Often the document has to be rewritten sometimes many times until all parties are happy and a final agreement can be reached.
- Often this can result in time delays because of the loss of drafts or the different versions of the agreement being out of synchronization with each other.

- Often there can be substantial delays with the document having to be transported to each party involved.
- There is also a real possibility of the loss of income because of time delays.
- Competitors or third parties have the opportunity to interfere or offer alternative deals because of the delay.
- There could be a loss of momentum or initial enthusiasm for the venture which could result in losing the opportunity.

When a business document is on blockchain:

- All the parties would be forced to have an open honest discussion, no shady details could be hidden.
- The whole document can be drawn up and edited with the consensus of all parties in real time.
- When an agreement is reached, the deal can be made. Money can be exchanged and goods dispatched immediately.

Over the last almost 30 years, the Internet has proven itself to be durable and practicable which sets a good foundation for blockchain technology to follow as it continues to develop.

One of the greatest attributes of blockchain is its ability to ensure everyone using it is forced to be accountable for their input and actions. The loss of information and opportunities that are caused because of missed transactions, mechanical, machine or even human errors, theft, fraud, imposters, scammers and confidence tricksters are eliminated with blockchain.

This is accomplished because blockchain records everything in a main register and also in the collective and connected blockchain registers that are distributed through the system to all users. There is built in robustness in blockchain in much the same way as on the Internet, it just does not have any single point where it can fail. There has not been any significant disruption of blockchain since it was first started in 2008.

Blockchain stores everything in blocks of information, each block being identical in every detail in every location or area, it has been or is currently being used or stored across the blockchain network.

It is not possible for a permission type database blockchain to be controlled by any solo or single entity. In order to change or alter any unit or block of information on blockchain, the whole network would need to be overridden. This could, in theory, be possible, but the reality is it is unlikely to happen. If someone decided to take control of the system to capture cyber currency, for example, such as bitcoins, this would result in them soon becoming worthless making the exercise pointless.

Chapter 3: How does Blockchain Work

Many people consider blockchain technology as the greatest invention since the Internet original was invented. This is because it allows people to exchange value simply, easily, without the need to trust anyone or take a gamble on being paid or receiving value for your money.

Blockchain databases for person to person distribution with time and date stamped input are managed autonomously, they allowed bitcoin to be the first digital or cryptocurrency to automatically remove the ability for double spending of the same money. This technology has inspired blockchain to be used in many different applications.

A very good and simple example of how blockchain works is if you decide to make a bet with someone:

Say you decide to make a bet that your favorite team will win the football game next Saturday.

You make a bet that if your team loses, you will pay $100 to the other person, they agree to bet that your team will lose and their team will win. If their team loses and your team wins, they will pay you $100.

There are several options you have to ensure the bet is honored.

1. Option one is you are both friends and trust each other so it is likely the loser will pay the debt, this may be the

simplest arrangement, but there is still the chance that your friend will not pay you.

2. You can draw up a legal contract, this usually ensures people will pay and fulfill their contract, but if they do not you have a legal remedy to get your money, this could be expensive and take a long time to get your money.

3. You could give the money to a third party to hold. The problem is they may decide to keep all the money themselves and not pay, disappearing with all of your money.

4. You could give the money to a bookie who will take a cut of the money for the trouble of doing it. This is usually a good method, but you could lose 20 to 30% or more in costs and commissions.

These are all options that involve trust and can be expensive if that trust is not kept.

Using the blockchain option is safe. You can write just a few lines of code into a program that runs on blockchain. Both of you use your cyber currency (such as bitcoin) to place your $100 dollars in the blockchain program. The program will keep the $200 safe until the results of the game on Saturday are known. It will then automatically check the results from many different sources and transfer the whole amount of the money, $200 to the person who wins the bet.

During the process, it is easy to monitor what is happening to both parties and even a third party can check the process and the contact arrangements. In fact, anyone can see what is happening, but the process cannot be stopped or changed, the winner will receive their $200.00.

This may seem a bit of a drama to go through over a small bet of $100, but exactly the same process can be used when buying a car, a house or investing your money anywhere. By using blockchain you have eliminated the risk of losing your money.

Walmart, one of the world's largest chain stores with branches in almost every city in the western world, has in association with IBM, been running blockchain trials to develop methods that will allow them to track and trace in real time the supply train of all their produce.

This makes it possible to see where and when produce was harvested, including the growing conditions and methods used (organics or not), as well as the storage and distribution pathways used by the different businesses and agents who handle it before it gets to your table.

To date, there have been many attempts to do this both by growers, manufacturers, health regulatory authorities and consumer groups. Unfortunately, it has proven to be extremely expensive and the results proved to be very inconsistent and questionable.

Using blockchain with the collaboration of all the people involved in all aspects of the food chain from the farmers right through to the consumer, this can be simplified and streamlined.

You will be able to go into a shop and read from the label that particular food item's history, confident that the information is true and correct.

When purchasing fish, for example, you would be able to tell if it is ocean caught or farmed.

If the fish was farmed, blockchain would have all the details from when it was a fingerling to the time it was harvested, including the types of feeds used and the water conditions of the farm it came from. These would be date stamped as would the journey from the farm to the consumer. You would know the details of the middlemen it passed through and if it was fresh or frozen.

If the fish was ocean caught, you could find out the date it was caught. The area, of which ocean it came from so you can be sure it was not caught in polluted or radiation contaminated waters. The information on whether it was instantly snapped-frozen or placed in an ice slurry and for how long, plus the handling and transportation details of how it came to you.

You could then, if it meets with your acceptance, elect to purchase it and place it into your shopping cart. A blockchain program would at that, by way of a smart reader automatically process your purchase and the grower, farmer or fisherman and all others who need to be paid up and down the supply chain would be directly credited.

This allows for hassle-free shopping with no need to wait in lines for checkout or worrying about the quality of your purchase.

Of course, this would demand the collaboration of all the people involved, but it is in their interests to cooperate as they, in being part of the program would then be able to receive the best possible price for their labors paid instantly.

I expect within a few years those who do not opt for using a similar system will find it very hard to compete except on a very local level.

It is estimated that over 90% of all goods that are shipped worldwide are done so in containers. Using blockchain to track the many millions of containers and their contents that traverse the oceans of the world, this difficult task is simplified.

When sending refrigerated goods from some parts of East Africa or Asia to Europe, there can be over 30 different organizations that these goods have to pass through. It has been estimated there can be as many as 200 communication/interactions needed between freight companies, distributors, growers, import agents, health departments, tax collectors and other government port authorities as well as a variety of other middlemen for a container of fresh or frozen goods.

Using blockchain, a system can be developed where everyone in the supply chain from sender to recipient would be able to view exactly where their goods were in the supply chain and almost their exact time of arrival.

All the customs documents, shipping bills, and other documents would be right there on the blockchain with each entity receiving their required payment automatically as the goods pass through.

This high level of transparency and openness would practically eliminate fraud and theft and well as cut down on waste and overall costs. Benefiting all parties involved and resulting in a reduced cost to the consumer.

Private equity markets are now starting to use blockchain to assist with transparency for all people concerned with these types of transactions. Up until now, the private equity market has been a laborious process, involving a lot of manual work to track and record all the information and document all the different organizations involved. Documents have needed to be taken back and forth before they are finally approved by everyone concerned.

The wine industry has its share of trouble with counterfeit wine supplies and accounts. It is suspected that over 25% of all global wine sales are now counterfeit or substandard.

There has been a lot of fake "fine wine" on sale at auctions, tricking the wealthy into buying these counterfeit products. Now with blockchain, it is possible to track a bottle of wine for its full journey through its own unique digital thumbprint.

It is possible to know all the details of the wine, including the grower and the weather during the grape growing season and many other factors that can help the connoisseur select their wines.

Some of the world's largest mining companies like BHP Billiton are now using "Ethereum" based blockchain, this is to keep track of their field samples. Something that was until recently done manually, a long and slow process.

Rock samples are taken over an area divided into a grid. Often the samples are taken a few meters apart in an area that can cover from a hector to several square miles. This means there are hundreds sometimes thousands of core samples taken.

All the samples have to be numbered and recorded. Using blockchain this whole process is much quicker and simpler, with the results of the sample's assay being added it gives a glowing picture of the area and its potential.

The diamond industry is another area where blockchain has proven invaluable, not only in helping to check the authenticity of diamonds and other precious stones, but to keep track of them as well. Diamond fraud has been a problem for years, with many counterfeit and conflict or blood diamonds flooding the market. The use of blockchain is bringing more transparency to the diamond trading industry, with a reliable way to digitally verify diamonds.

Chapter 4: The Pros and Cons of Blockchain

There is a lot of confusion about the difference between "blockchain" and "bitcoin" mainly because blockchain was originally developed as a means to carry bitcoin or cyber currency safely. With the two of them so closely linked at the beginning, many people have become accustomed to using their names interchangeably without appreciating the difference.

To clarify, a little, thinking of Blockchain as a car or train and bitcoin as the passenger, may help.

So far I have provided some of the positive sides of blockchain such as its transparency, convenience, safety, removal of middlemen, and verification of information. Another benefit of blockchain is that transactions are irreversible. Going back to the example of you and your friend betting $100 on a football game, neither of you could change your mind and reverse the transaction when you realize your team is losing.

There are, as is to be expected, a few things against it. The one that is most apparent is the fact that once you enter any information into a block it is no longer private, it may still be your intellectual property and you retain all rights to it, but everyone and anyone who has access can view it and use the information.

The benefit of blockchain transactions being irreversible can also be considered a disadvantage. If there are fraudulent transactions made through your account, there is no way to reverse the transactions like you could easily do with a credit card.

Another problem with blockchain is the processing time, especially with large blocks, although this problem is expected to be resolved as blockchain develops.

Blockchain can be used to accommodate a wide range of applications, but it is divided into two types, a permission type database or an open or uncontrolled database.

Bitcoin and other cyber currency types of blockchain are totally uncontrolled. Anyone can read a block in the chain and likewise, anyone can write a new block into an existing chain.

A permission blockchain, on the other hand, is private like a centralized database, it can be owned or rather controlled by its originator. The network often referred to as the protocol can be set so that only those who have been given the correct codes can read or write on or in the database. There can be full permission or partial permission granted, depending on the codes provided.

For people who are only worried about confidentiality in their databases and are not concerned with trust issues, then at the present time blockchain has no real advantage over conventional or centralized databases or the Internet as we know it today.

Anyone who tries to hide their information in an uncontrolled blockchain needs to know some very advanced cryptographic and similar computer skills to achieve this and the effort is just not worthwhile as the information can easily just be placed in a private database that is not connected to the Internet.

The whole question of Internet security is complex and it is usually hard to tell the difference between someone who is doing a bit of harmless browsing, surfing the net or just doing research for an article and a potential thief. There are a lot of people using the net at any one time, so it is almost impossible to catch single fraudsters. Which is why a secure incorruptible blockchain is a very good idea!

Mostly the people who do get caught in dishonest acts on the Internet are people who are running large scale pirating operations over an extended period, making them easy to trace compared with small time or once only fraudsters.

Blockchain in itself is very secure in that everything done on blockchain is out in the open and can be seen in real time. All the information is traceable and not able to be removed, altered or tampered with.

There has been a lot of talk about blockchain theft and fraud, almost all of this is because people have tried to use blockchain as a pyramid scheme or they have not been careful to secure their access code or blockchain digital key.

Chapter 5: Cryptocurrency

Cryptocurrency is just a term used to describe the method of payment or digital currency that can be sent or exchanged using the Internet without going through a bank or other financial institution.

The term node is given to the application of a computer connected to a blockchain network. When blocks are added to a blockchain they always get added in a linear and chronological order. The node checks, validates and relays the transactions or information automatically and gets a copy of the current blockchain when joining the net.

In a real sense, each node is an administrator of the blockchain, it overseas the joining to the network and is encouraged by its program to do so because in doing so it can win bitcoins. This is called "mining bitcoins", this is a very clever idea where the node competes with other nodes to solve computer puzzles and win bitcoins (or a percentage of one). This is the original reason bitcoins were conceived, not so much as a cryptocurrency as they now are, but to encourage the blockchain to operate and expand.

As soon as it was developed many new potential uses or applications for this technology started to be investigated.

The actual value of cryptocurrency is not controlled in the same way as the US dollar or any other country's currency, neither is it controlled by the World Bank, any central banks or institutions. The value of this form of currency is directly determined by the network of people using the same cryptocurrency.

When someone decides to use cryptocurrency either by sending or receiving, they are accepting the currency as a totally valid form of payment. When this happens it gives a perceived and recognized value to the cryptocurrency.

The reality is there is no such thing as a bitcoin, you cannot hold it in your hand or even see it, it is just a term used to convey a value. This value is recorded in a public ledger system called a blockchain. This ledger keeps track of a list of addresses and how many units (or values) are recorded at those addresses on an ever-expanding list.

If you are the owner of bitcoin, you do not have a physical coin, what you own is a private cryptographic key that will unlock a specific address. If you were to print out your key it would be a long string of letters, numbers, and symbols.

The security of your key or this line of numbers is the bitcoin's only weakness, making it imperative that you keep it or them secure if you have more than one.

Most people advise you to keep copies of your key secured in several different hard to find or reach places. Some of the most secure places to keep a copy would be in a paper printout placed in a safety deposit box at a bank or a reputable banking institution. Storing your key on a hard drive or USB stick that is not and never is online, is a good option and there are online services that offer to secure your key, but several of these have been corrupted or gone broke, disappearing with the key codes of many peoples bitcoins.

Whichever method or methods you decide to use, always make sure you have multiple levels of security, but be aware that all methods can be vulnerable. With the huge growth in value of all cryptocurrencies, it is starting to become more important as the value of each bitcoin is increasing, expeditiously. What started a few years ago at under a dollar for a bitcoin is now worth over $8,000 USD. This makes bitcoin a very valuable commodity.

One thing to be aware of is Bitcoin is volatile. It reached a value above $19,000 USD in December of 2017 and as of April 2018, it is now worth $8,000 USD. The prices of bitcoin drop and rise fairly quickly. In just the month of April, the price has gone from $6,000 USD to $8,000 USD.

Bitcoin sounds like the ideal place to store and manage illicit or illegal money, but in practice, it is not. Most people on the black market and those dealing in stolen property do not want to have their business in such an obvious and open situation where all the details become public.

An illegal drug bazaar called "Sheep Marketplace," that was used to keep the details and private bitcoin keys that belonged to a large number of people involved in drug dealing and other illegal activities was recently attacked and plundered. The thieves got away with over $100 million worth of cryptocurrency, stolen from their customers. It is unclear because of the illegal nature of the operation and the fact that for obvious reasons they're not wanting to involve the authorities, just who was responsible for this attack, but it appears that it was an inside job.

Most cryptocurrency attacks and certainly the most lucrative ones are made against online services that people use to store the details of their private keys. Often these services hold the keys for a large number of clients. An insider would have little work to do if trying to hack into and find, then copy the keys in all the databases. They would then have control of all the bitcoins or other cryptocurrencies until the owner moves the currency elsewhere, they would lose control.

The first known bitcoin heist happened in June 2011, when Allinvain had about half a million dollars of bitcoins stolen overnight. There have been many instances of fraud involving bitcoin since then. Some are cases of outright theft, while others like "Bitcoin Savings & Trust," a firm that portrayed themselves as being a high return investment opportunity, company, when in fact they were only a pyramid scheme. When caught the owners were charged with fraud and stealing over $4.5 million from their investors. "MyBitcoin", a so-called electronic wallet service for safely storing peoples' bitcoin keys, just disappeared with over a million dollars worth of its user's bitcoins.

Some of the most trusted and well known bitcoin companies like "MT. Gox" and "Bitcoinica", (Biticionica is now out of business) suffered high-profile thefts.

Cryptocurrencies are like cash, but once a transaction is made the only way to get stolen cryptocurrency back is to physically track down the thief and force them to repay you, which is why it is attractive to thieves. With credit card thieves, you can cancel your card and reverse the fraudulent transaction, a luxury that you do not have with cryptocurrency.

It is very difficult for most people to really grasp exactly how digital fraud happens. Most people would not know just what they were stealing if they tried and if they managed to get it, they would not know how to use it!

The biggest problem with such things as blockchain and cryptocurrency like bitcoin is that the people using them often do not really understand what they are doing, so they are forced to use intermediaries.

One of the huge advantages of blockchain is that it should not need intermediaries or middlemen. In fact, that is a major reason it is so attractive to many people and businesses.

So the key to successfully using blockchain and cryptocurrency is to learn about it so you can work it independently.

If the owners of these bitcoins that were stolen in the examples above had properly secured their digital keys instead of allowing them to be looked after by businesses that were themselves not secure, (as proven by the robberies) they could not have been robbed.

Blockchain is going to take a while until it becomes acceptable to the mainstream Internet users due to the amount of bad publicity it has enjoyed and because of its complexity.

Bitcoin is not accepted as a means of payment by the majority of banking institutions or online checkout operations yet, but many websites are beginning to accept bitcoin and many more might in the near future.

Some sites like Newegg will accept bitcoin and it is possible to use downloadable processors like "Stripe Payment Processor" to have online merchants accept bitcoin, but they will not take any other type of cryptocurrency. This is expected to change very soon as it appears many financial institutions are racing to be the first to embrace this new technology and become leaders in this field.

Chapter 6: Investing in Cryptocurrency

If you want to successfully invest in cryptocurrency, then you really need to understand a bit about blockchain and cryptocurrency to be able to make a realistically informed and good decision before investing. You do not need to be able to write computer code or learn computer programing and enter the world of the nerd, but a basic understanding of the principles is necessary.

Bitcoin and Ethereum are the two leading and hottest investment opportunities currently available. This could of course change as new cryptocurrencies are developed. They are riding on essentially the expectation that they will soon become a non-manipulable money used by the whole world.

The people advocating their use suggest they will soon take over from the Dollar, Pound, Euro and Yen, and other major trading currencies to become the first free world currency.

If you hold bitcoin shares then you can be part of and gain financially from this venture. If or when Bitcoin or Ethereum start to replace the monetary reserves of country's reserve banks or become the dominant currencies for the world and international trade their value will become many times what it is today. There is also a great possibility that this will never happen.

The website www.coinmarketcap.com has a list of over 1000 cryptocurrencies where you can review their price, market cap, volume, circulating supply, and price change within the past 24 hours.

The investment history of cryptocurrencies is easy to follow, bitcoin has had a huge increase since the bubble in 2011 where a bitcoin was worth less than $20 USD. Now a bitcoin is valued at over $8,000 USD as of April 2018.

In terms of investment return, this is incredible and sounds almost too good to be true, but it is a fact. The question is, will it continue on its upward curve and increase further or will the bubble burst and leave investors out of pocket. (Many broken and bankrupt)

The answer is it could go either way, but is likely to keep rising for the foreseeable future for several reasons

- The possibility of war between North Korea and the US.
- The lack of confidence in most countries' currency and the expectation of another collapse of dollar values.
- The large amount of natural disasters striking the world, for example, the drought in California and storms in southern US, Caribbean and many parts of Asia.
- The Muslim and refugee problems in Europe.

Cryptocurrencies are not ordinary investments and by and large not regulated and controlled by government regulations (at least not yet because they are still in the development stage). They are considered a high risk investment and should not be entered into lightly.

As most people who are just becoming aware of blockchain and its potential will be thinking "I should have invested in this a couple of years ago when a bitcoin was only a dollar, now it's worth over $8,000 USD." If we all knew 10 years ago what we know today well....

It is not too late to catch this "gravy train" and make substantial amounts of money **BUT** be aware of the risks and understand what you are doing first.

Being a high risk investment they are causing a bit of concern in some circles, with some governments and large financial institutions who are looking to protect themselves trying to outlaw some aspects of blockchain.

If they are successful (and they hold a tremendous amount of persuasive power), this could outlaw cryptocurrencies, posing a risk to investors, but (and this is also very likely) it could backfire on them and just force cryptocurrency underground, driving their value even higher.

The only time anyone should invest any money in anything is when that money they are using is surplus to their requirements and if losing it, will not matter.

Do not invest the money you need to live on and provide the necessities for your family.

It's foolish for anyone to own any investment they cannot afford to lose.

But it is definitely a good idea to invest at least some of their nonessential money in Bitcoin, Ethereum, or any other cryptocurrency of their choice.

OK, so now the reasons why:

- The dollar is probably heading for a fall, most people will tell you it has to happen again sooner or later. These things go in cycles.
- The technology is good and it is improving all the time.
- To support the idea of a free money system and get rid of all the corrupt politicians, large Multinational Companies and Rothschild type Bankers.
- This has the possibility of solving much of the conflicts in the world and evenly distributing the wealth.
- You could make a substantial amount of money.

And the risks and reason to avoid

- This is new technology and all the players are inexperienced, with a lot of unknown and unproven players. Cryptocurrency brokers should be viewed as a lot more risky than secondhand car dealers or offshore binary options brokers.

  So, if and when you buy, move everything to your own wallet and deal from there, leaving as little as possible with brokers.

- It is really a good idea to understand what you are buying and some of the technical aspects. Blockchain and cryptocurrency were created by super nerds. These people think on a different level to the way many people do. This has resulted in a blockchain that is often not very user-friendly.

  An example of this is:

  I did not study medicine, I am not a doctor so when I get sick, I go to the doctor to be diagnosed and cured. I do not try to be my own doctor and medicate myself. It is the same with blockchain either go to someone who knows like a blockchain professional or do a lot of research and learn for yourself (the best option).

- There is a possibility that some of this new technology will fail or be drastically changed, a type of natural, technological evolution, so everything needs to be watched carefully and spread your investment.

- There is a word in crypto language FOMO which means "the Fare of Missing Out". Do not fall for it, it is for suckers and sneaky salesmen. If you are thinking this then you are ready to become an easy target for sweet talking scammers who will strip you bare of your cash and be gone without a trace.

The best approach for the novice is to buy a small amount of Bitcoin or Ethereum, you can buy as little as $1 or 1 €, £, ¥ or equivalent in your local currency and play with it, see how it works and what it can do. Check the charts and compute where it's going and get a real feel for it. If you lose, it is a small price to pay for a good lesson. If you had invested a large amount you would have lost that too. Be realistic, live within your budget/means.

Then you will be able to buy some more and slowly build up your investment when your confidence and knowledge allows you to do so with relatively little risk.

It is important to be aware that although blockchain has now been around for a few years, it is still developing and is constantly evolving. There will be a lot of different approaches trying to make it commercially viable, so it is to be expected a few of them will not work out.

Prudence, as well as a lot of trial and error experimenting, will need to be gone through while the different products either become used or obsolete. Investors will have to spread their interests over a wide range of areas, with the expectation that some areas will gain and some will lose to be able to find the greatest profits overall.

It is well worth looking at a range of cryptocurrencies that are tied to decentralized services that give more than providing a set store value. Bitcoin is and will probably remain the king, but Ethereum is much more than just a currency, it fuels entire networks of decentralized organizations as well as smart contracts.

Several places to start looking at when thinking about having a diversified blockchain investment are projects that are aimed at decentralized and encrypted cloud storage and those that are geared to allow you to lease the unused processing space and power of your own cloud space and that on your computer. The reason these are likely to become a very good investment is that they are still affordable investments.

When you buy cryptocurrency, it is best to store your private keys in what's called a hardware wallet or cold wallet. People also refer to it as a hard wallet, short for hardware wallet. These wallets are similar to flash drives that safely store your private keys offline and can be connected to a computer whenever needed to make a transaction.

Hot wallets or soft wallets, on the other hand, store your private keys online through a third party such as Coinbase, Blockchain.info, Electrum, etc. The problem with storing your private keys in a soft wallet is the possibility of the third party getting hacked. This is what happened with Mt. Gox. Some people stored their private keys in Mt. Gox and when Mt. Gox apparently got hacked, their customers lost all their bitcoins.

The paper wallet is considered the safest wallet though less convenient than a hard wallet. This is literally a document in which you write down or print barcodes of all your private keys and store it somewhere safe. Some people may argue that this is the best wallet to have rather than a hard wallet.

The top two hard wallets as of early 2018 are Ledger Nano S and Trezor. Trezor is a bit more expensive than the Ledger Nano S but both have great reviews by cryptocurrency holders. There are other hard wallets you can easily find online through a simple google search if you're interested in other options.

Chapter 7: Blockchain's effect on Technology

Blockchain has the potential to make small scale as well as much larger projects viable by drastically reducing the amount of paperwork and double handling of information involved.

The ability to have decentralized networks that are self-sufficient and can be integrated with any other network as needed are going to completely reshape the way technologies are implemented in the future.

A good example is a home-based or small commercial energy production system using solar panels and or turbines combined with Blockchain technology and Ethereum based smart contracts.

These contracts are able to redistribute the power you generate when you have extra to the national grid or into the local micro-grid supply. Then, when necessary purchase electricity when you require.

The smart contracts add and subtract the energy as it is consumed or generated and automatically adjust your power account accordingly in what is now referred to as a smart or intelligent grid.

Similar Ethereum-based smart contracts can work with many other types of applications, giving a variety of new business opportunities as a result of blockchain, by giving all Internet users an ability for creating value from digital information.

Any company you deal with can instantly be checked with blockchain, it becomes totally transparent and all its actions are verifiable including ownership, integrity, digital assets, information, and equity.

Smart contracts can be created and executed with a simple code when certain specified conditions are met. These have the potential of changing dramatically the way many people do business. An example, it could be agreed that payments are made when a financial negotiation or instrument meets certain predetermined conditions.

Many new types of arrangements such as share riding in vehicles as an alternative to taking taxis need an intermediary such as Uber to connect people who want to ride with drivers. Blockchain makes it easier for these types of arrangements as it allows for direct interaction between interested parties. Blockchain can also provide a clear, no fuss payment system making it a truly decentralized economic sharing system.

Many people are becoming increasingly more concerned about some of the claims companies make regarding their products. Consumers are now requiring that ethical methods are used in growing, manufacturing and the processing of food items as well as other everyday products.

Using blockchain you can check that your local restaurant is using fresh ocean caught seafood not cheap toxic fish from Asian fish farms. The wine you're drinking is really from Matu Valley Nelson, NZ and that the vegetables used as well as the bread is made with organic GM free produce.

With blockchain the political system becomes an open book with Politicians, at last, being open to public scrutiny. They would not be able to hide their assets and interests, all the conditions of being elected and their promises would be public knowledge. Bribes and backhanders along with conflicting interests would become instantly apparent.

Elections could be simplified and the public voice would be heard throughout the term of office of all elected officials, making them accountable.

The education system could be totally reformed with the majority of people having the choice of formal schooling or home style school.

The medical system would finally be brought under control with patients, hospitals and doctors all being accountable for their actions or inactions.

The general population would benefit because using a blockchain system, the taxation of everyone would be better controlled without the possibility of people or companies evading their tax obligations.

It would no longer be possible for people to abuse the social welfare system. Pensions and benefits would go to those who qualify and those abusing the system would be excluded. Social welfare could not be abused and those in need would be assured of the help they are entitled to.

Chapter 8: Blockchain and the Finance Industry

One of the biggest problems with working on the Internet is a person or company's' ability to prove their credentials. Verifying your identity is the key to being able to make or be part of financial transactions and other interactions that happen on the Internet. Internet fraud is a huge problem and in underdeveloped countries, it can be a huge financial nightmare, not only for individuals but for businesses as well.

Blockchain is able to minimize the risks associated with dealing with people on the net, not only locally, but nationally and internationally. The enhanced methods used by blockchain with the automatic verification processes and digitized personal documentation would allow people to have a secure identity and check the identity of those they are dealing with instantly without any fuss or inconvenience.

With the new concepts of sharing economies and increasingly cashless society that is starting to favor bartering and exchanges for goods or services rendered, being able to instantly prove who you are is becoming more important.

One of the areas that many people are concerned about when providing personal information anywhere on the net is, "just what their information may be used for".

Many social media platforms or sites such as Facebook, Twitter, Instagram, LinkedIn and all the other free sites gather vast amounts of information from all their users, often this information is not of a personal nature and is not traceable back to the individual user. Rather, it is used for large companies and organizations, including governments, to gauge all manner of public opinion and market trends.

The amount of information taken from each individual post or Internet interaction is very small, its value on an individual basis is so small it is not possible for it to be reasonably measured or calculated by today's monetary system. But using blockchain it becomes realistic, in the not too distant future, while using any online system you will have the ability to control, sell and manage any data or income your online activities may generate automatically.

This can happen because blockchain with systems such as bitcoin can operate using fractional amounts. Especially with increased and high volume users these very small amounts can add up and become of merit. It is a little bit like being paid to take surveys, each survey to take, only gives a few cents, but over time it can add up.

Cryptographic techniques are used to make individual data based calculations and build intricate bulk computations. These can be over individuals or over segments and groups of the population to provide information that is a saleable commodity.

Many people have experienced some difficult situations while trying to work on the Internet. Blockchain allows everyone to transfer any piece of digital property they wish to any other Internet user in a safe and secure way. The fact that this transfer has taken place becomes public knowledge and nobody can challenge its legitimacy, an important fact.

Stock and share trading is another area where blockchain has the potential to add more efficiency, both in time and reducing costs. Using blockchain, all transactions can be instantaneous, with confirmation and payment and total settlement happening together. The need for clearing house, auditors and custodians are removed, they just are not needed, resulting in greater profits for the individual.

Many stock and commodities exchanges throughout the world are now searching for ways to hold their lucrative markets and prototyping blockchain applications for the different services they offer. They have now recognized they need to diversify into other areas to survive.

Chapter 9: Blockchain & Enhanced Security

Everyone now recognized that the Internet has security problems from annoying spam mail to unscrupulous persons holding people's websites and personal computers for ransom with different viruses and superbugs. Because it stores data across its network, the blockchain eliminates the potential risks that come with data being held centrally. This lack of centralized points of vulnerability means that hackers cannot exploit your computer.

The reliance on username/password type systems to protect our assets and identity online are eliminated because blockchain uses encryption technology that cannot be hacked.

Blockchain uses public and private keys, to store your data in an incorruptible block.

The private key works like a password and the public key is your address on the blockchain. Although blockchain is incorruptible, its weakness (this needs to be stressed, which is why I keep repeating it) is your private key, so print it out and keep it in a paper wallet (an envelope somewhere very safe).

Right now only about half the world has access or knows how to use the Internet, but that is changing very quickly, there are over a million new, first time users every day coming online and the web is currently overloaded, blockchain will be able to capitalize on this because its decentralized websites have the ability to speed up file transfer with faster streaming times while protecting users' information from getting hacked or lost.

Protecting your intellectual property has become a problem for many copyright holders who have found it very difficult to keep control of their intellectual property and losing financially as a consequence. With a few clicks, any digital information can easily be copied and distributed because of the Internet.

Blockchain and smart contracts have the ability to eliminate unauthorized file copying and protect copyright by automating the sale of intellectual property and creative works online, this includes music, books, photos and movies.

Chapter 10: The Government and the Legality of Blockchain

Because blockchain is relatively new and has had little impact on business and commerce, there are no laws that directly relate to it, only general laws of privacy and copyright. This will change when its impact starts to be felt to any degree. Especially if every big financial institution and those that control big business interests work out how they can control and possibly monopolize it.

An area that has for a long time been susceptible to different kinds of fraud, is different land ownership and land title issues. This also includes issues such as inheritance and dual ownership of properties as well as leasehold. These have always been a difficult and sometimes costly as well as a labor intensive area to administer to.

Blockchain and smart contracts can eliminate many of these problems because it cannot be corrupted.

It is going to take some time before the majority of people become aware of blockchain and the implications it could have on them.

Whatever happens with it, there as always will have to be a tradeoff between the benefits and people's privacy.

It seems that the next step in the blockchain evolution could quite possibly be a world where money as we know it is no longer relevant or necessary.

One thing that is certain is the banking and financial sector as well as all the other intermediaries that have been living off the productive members of society are going to have to reform.

Conclusion

Thank you for reading my book on "Understanding Blockchain Technology and Cryptocurrency." I hope it has given you some insight on how this fascinating new technology works and it has answered some of the questions you may have about it.

Blockchain is a new type of technology that everyone needs to look into as it is going to dominate how things will be done in the future.

Of course, you can just go with the flow and let one of the greatest opportunities you are ever likely to find just pass you by, and for some, that may be for the best.

But for those who wish to become financially independent and provide a sound future not only for themselves and their children, but also for their generations that will follow in the future, then I would suggest that you take the time to invest in your future.

That does not mean to just madly buy up as many bitcoins as possible, which is not a sound way to go. In fact, that is the road to disaster.

Take a conservative approach and ignore all the hype, those that are shouting the loudest are most likely scammers and fraudsters. Just be aware that the value of cryptocurrency such as bitcoin is rising up drastically and quickly, but still take the time to do research on it first.

Before you buy any cryptocurrencies online, be sure to check them out thoroughly first. This can be done by googling their name and reading their reviews. If they are legitimate, then there will good reports. Follow these and ensure they are real, then make a choice. Remember, it is very easy to separate a fool and his money, but hard to take anything from a careful, honest man or woman.

Access your surplus assets, and determine how much you can safely afford to spend without having to worry if you lose it as you possibly will, then divide that in two and use that to buy some cryptocurrency.

View this as a learning curve and try your own and other people's theories, some will work and some will be disappointing. These types of investments are very similar to investing in land, sometimes the market drops and you can lose 20 or 30% percent (or more) of the value. But if you are there for a quick dollar then you might not seem to be getting anywhere. Those in for the long haul know that non-deteriorating assets like land, gold and shares in technology are very unlikely to drop.

An example, a man had a property that he purchased in 1984 for $10,000. He was offered $35,000 for it 3 years later, so he sold it, thinking he made a good profit. Then six months later the property market took a dive and it was resold for $20,000. He thought how lucky he was for selling it before the market went down. Now that property is worth over 1 million dollars, so who was lucky?

The future of blockchain and cryptocurrency technology is very positive and it promises to directly influence almost every area of future business as well as personal life.

There is so much interest now from all types of business, covering a huge range of industries that with just their interest, it is pushing and stimulating more enterprises to try and develop the necessary blockchain networks to cope with the expected demand of the near future.

If you found this book helpful in any way would you please leave a review on Amazon?